The // Wonder // of // Seeing // Double

MANKATO STATE UNIVERSITY
MEMORIAL LIBRARY
MANKATO, MINNESOTA

The // Wonder // of // Seeing // Double

POEMS

ROBERT B. SHAW

THE UNIVERSITY OF MASSACHUSETTS PRESS

AMHERST

1988

Copyright © 1988 by Robert B. Shaw
All rights reserved
Printed in the United States of America
LC 88-1072
ISBN 0-87023-637-7 (cloth); 638-5 (paper)
Printed by Thomson-Shore and bound by John Dekker & Sons

Library of Congress Cataloging-in-Publication Data
Shaw, Robert Burns, 1947–
The wonder of seeing double : poems / Robert B. Shaw.
p. cm.
ISBN 0-87023-637-7 (alk. paper). ISBN 0-87023-638-5
(pbk. : alk. paper)
I. Title.
PS3569.H3845W6 1988   88-1072
811'.54—dc19   CIP

British Library Cataloguing in Publication
data are available

For Catherine and Tony

Contents

// I //

Narcissus 3
Family Album 4
Turning In 6
Waiting in the Wings 7
Bright Enough to See Your Face In 9
To the Cricket 11
Extended Run 12
Cloudscape 13
The Shortcut 14
Turn, Turn 15
Out Back in the Evening 16
Note Found in a Room in a Summer Hotel 17
Coast Patrol 21
Contemporary Music 22
Old Burying Ground 24
Half-Holiday 26
Things We Will Never Know 28
Chronometrics 30
Moss 36
Partial Draft 37
Last Winter 38
Homework 39
Accidents 40

// II //

Echo 43
Circumlocution 44
Some Methods of Going to Sleep 46
There and Back Again 47

The Voice of the Yawn   49
Safe Harbor   50
Spring's Awakening   51
The Floater   52
The Invention of Zero   53
Acclimatizing   54
The Crossing   55
Early Natural History   56
Their Voices   58
Blues Remembered   59
Ash Wednesday, Late Afternoon   60
Souvenir   61
A Late Greeting Card   62
A Time Piece   63
Morning Exercise   64
Finding Words   65
To the Next Tenants   66
Just Here and Now   68

Acknowledgments

Acknowledgment is made to the editors of the following publications in which several of the poems in this book first appeared:

Blue Moon: "Their Voices," "Finding Words"
Kenyon Review: "Old Burying Ground," "Homework," "Extended Run"
The New Republic: "The Invention of Zero"
PN Review: "Coast Patrol," "The Voice of the Yawn," "Turn, Turn," "Acclimatizing"
Paris Review: "Out Back in the Evening"
Partisan Review: "The Floater," "Cloudscape"
Poetry: "Partial Draft," "Moss," "Early Natural History," "Chronometrics," "Narcissus," "Echo," "Family Album," "Things We Will Never Know," "Safe Harbor," "Spring's Awakening"
The Yale Review: "Blues Remembered," "Just Here and Now," "There and Back Again"

"Turning In" was issued as a broadside by Pharos Books. "To the Cricket" appeared in *Sotheby's International Poetry Competition 1982 Anthology,* and "Contemporary Music" appeared in *The Observer & Ronald Duncan Foundation Poetry Competition 1985 Anthology.*

I wish to thank the National Endowment for the Arts for its support in the final phase of assembling this collection. I wish to record as well my gratitude to the late Robert Fitzgerald for help and encouragement over many years. In the poem "To the Cricket" the translation into English of the insect's song is by him.

// I //

Narcissus

This match was made in heaven, or let's say
confected in a patch of fallen sky
idling under your avid contemplation,
hot young hunter here pinned to the brink
of waters you once hunkered down to drink.
How long ago was that? There's no before,
no after, all's a privileged moment snared
in cool solution, not precipitating
even beneath your gripped and melting gaze.
Here is the end. The end will be to see
all and yet never enough in one pale face
looking helplessly up as you lean down
and the woods drift from gray to green to brown.
Never to heed or hasten or grow old,
no eye for the new leaf timidly unfolding,
nor for the sun that broadly winks in passing
over your acne-pitted shoulder at
the object floating unattained and chaste
as that sweet medium for ever holding
still, as still as it can, for your slow take.
No echo sounds. How can the hunt be over?
The dream will not be told until you wake.
What would it take, a magic word to free you,
letting the figure loose to join the flow?
All you can do is let the lover see you,
having long ceased to listen, speak, or know.

Family Album

Some fiddling with the lens,
some flattery with the light—
and Smile! We smile. Snap!
Our smiles, deft as wrens,
clearing the shutter flap,
take roost within the little box of night.

Latent on celluloid,
our likenesses await
favorable developments:
unviewed, their spell is void.
Must we amass evidence—
hems or hair, wedding rings we can date—

that things aren't as they were?
Evidently we must.
Jarring our own focus, Time's
remodelings make a blur,
scenes of his petty crimes
fast fading but for curatorial lust

to clutch at what we know
did not, could never last.
Embalmed in silver salts,
our former selves are slow
to anger, kind to faults,
look up with hope, forgiving all that's past.

"Look, I was thinner then."
"That must have been the year
they cut the maple down."
"Which one of her young men
was that?" "Just some poor clown."
"There's the old tractor Uncle let you steer." . . .

Snap the book shut. Our seeing
will never match the flash
that riveted these frail,
fluttering plumes of being.
Blinking aside detail,
the eye that masters tear and lid and lash

mimes rather that machine
(the Brownie's graver kin)
that scorns the surface clay
as did the shrouded Dean,
loosing a cold, lightless ray
to probe the pile of chalk that waits within.

Turning In

Moving from room to room, flipping off lights,
yawning a little, at last turning down the heat,
I see myself flash by in mirrors and more
obscurely in the black unflattering panes
I pause at hand upheld to lower shades.
In the hall I look for longer than I intended
through the bevel-edged glass of the front door
at a neighbor's second or possibly third car,
parked as need would have it on the street.
A sugary coat of frost has made of this
compact unglamorous heap a gleaming trinket,
a stocking-stuffer some tycoon
ordered out of a catalogue for a playmate.
I shoot the dead bolt. Wind chisels under the door.
I turn the porch light off and find myself
nose to nose with the lusterless image that may
show truer in its way than the mirror's gloss.
I cannot think of anything more recent
than ten years ago, or of any place
not miles away from this place,
and I find myself saying something almost true:
no one who knew me then would know me now.

Waiting in the Wings

Here we are for the hundred-and-tenth performance;
the leading man, downstage, is mixing cocktails
and flickering glances at the ingenue
prettily posed beside a vase of flowers,
calculating how many drams will do
to keep the evening flowing in planned channels.
I see this from the sidelines, trading weight
from one to another haunch on a hard chair.
This is the sort of touring company
where everyone except the star does chores;
I am the understudy not yet needed,
meanwhile the prompter that he never needs.
I do admire him. I realize more each night
how much resides in gesture. See the swish
he gives the martini pitcher (full of water,
as everyone wills to forget, and ice cubes made
of durable plastic, as perhaps fewer realize).
Look at his three-quarter turn to her, his thumb
nesting under the sash of his smoking jacket.
Costumes went over budget at some point:
there's only one such covetable bit
of old-wine-bottle-green glad rags.
But we are of a size. Were he to have
a fainting fit or a heart attack, they'd strip it
gently from his limp frame and stuff me into it.
And then I would be ON.
      No more of that.
Sitting with script in hand I notice what
a way he has with words. He makes them up
often enough, sometimes ten lines together
come out of nowhere framed in full aplomb.
But even when they're lines I have before me
like some disputed contract on my lap,
his lithe delivery does them something more
than justice, the words paced, the accents placed
like cat feet padding nimbly down a fence rail.

Would you, would I, would anyone have said
those lines the way he did a moment back?
"Darling, let's not ever discuss money.
I think of it as . . . the least of my attractions."
Masterly, the positioning of that pause;
I'd have rushed through it, putting one over on her.
But he, although he knows that *she's* the heiress,
mingles his irony and self-esteem
in subtly measured parts, with, as it were,
the pitcher's final swish as he glides toward her.
It's no surprise he gets her in the end,
nor that she thinks *he's* the acquisition.

Ho hum. One act to go. The only acting
I've done this trip was in the greasy spoon
across the street last night. The new young waitress
was certain I must be the leading man.
She brought my coffee, asked for an autograph.
I signed a place mat with his name, and even
dotted the i with a sort of little star.
It somehow seemed too easy. So I said,
"You know that it's a stage name," wrote my own
right name beneath his wrong one. Then I paid
with a five dollar bill, told her to keep the change,
calming her flustered thanks over my shoulder
with "Darling, let's not ever discuss money."
That was it, at last, best of both worlds.
And even then it somehow seemed too easy—
would have even without the screen door's clapping
shut with such a curt vocational comment.
I came back feeling not so much disposed
to drop a sandbag on him. When the tour
bows out for good in the last sad prairie town
I'll step across the footlights, take a column,
crowd the press rows with the other critics.
A critic is the artist's guilty conscience,
skewering what he knows to be too easy
with that uneasy instrument, his pen.
I think you'd say I have a talent for it.

Bright Enough to See Your Face In

Twice a year she polished "the old silver."
This was a ceremony that demanded
towels spread out at one end of the table,
basins of soapy water and clear water,
many soft cloths, the squat jar of polish,
and, lined up for exacting treatment, things
we lived with day by day and never looked at:
the teapot hardly any company
was grand enough to merit, napkin rings
(only two: the children's were just wood),
the little tray *her* grandmother had used
for calling cards, which some unthinking piety
kept sitting unemployed in the front hall,
a child's mug which was, at least, employed
(used to hold toothpicks),—and the family spoons,
brought from the rack that held two rows of ten.
(An upper row of ten, a bottom row
of nine after a genteel kleptomaniac,
late of the Altar Guild, had made her move.)

Peering at each piece critically, she washed
and rinsed and dried it, then swabbed polish on.
It was a pink paste, and I used to think
the smell of it was pink—whatever that meant.
It wasn't pink for long; a little rubbing
made it the color of February slush
as it took every smudge unto itself.
Household magic! From a final flourish
issued a buffed-to-dazzling retinue,
ready to be set back on shelves, the spoons
hung by their bowls again to dangle proudly
handles crammed with curlicued initials.
Too good to use, they'd hang there good for nothing

but to amaze us six months further on
by how distinctly dingy they'd become,
taking on a gradual dusk of tarnish
by tinges too insidious to be noticed
till it was time to bring them down again.

She fought it back so many years, the stealthy
challenge of shadow, steady-paced corrosion
hovering in the very air we breathed.
How long is it since nineteen ovals winked
in idle brilliance at the plunging sun?
The bright idea I had of writing this
itself turns darker at the thought of time,
wearily searching for the single spoon
no pointed hints could ever conjure back
to join its showy fellows on the rack.
And where's the rack? What niece or nephew has it?
Two or three spoons that ended up with me
lie in some dresser somewhere, out of sight.
"If it's worth doing, it's worth doing right,"
she'd say, every six months, when she was done.
It isn't worth it, though, to everyone.
Sooner or later everyone gets robbed.

To the Cricket

Seducer, can your song
persist, keyed-up and long
as this unsleeping night?
The notion that it might,
that a spondaic chirr
is all that may occur
until the daylight rouses
birds in their penthouses—
the thought alone would keep
the mind astray from sleep.

Outdoors, but all too near
to an unwilling ear,
the friction of your knees
breeds importunities.
Please please meet me—your cry
wheedles each passerby
to be a pampered guest
in a snug ivy nest.
For ever pitched the same,
you are immune to shame,
and never chirp the less
for nightlong unsuccess.

Is it the cleaner choice
not to give need a voice?
Your silent auditor
finds second thoughts a bore,
yet fields them even while
framing a chilly smile,
counting the hours gone
and yet to go till dawn,
glad to the point of fear
that none will ever hear
his wants—unweakening, vain—
confessed to counterpane.

Extended Run

Across the road a ragged stand of trees
putting out summer growth puts out of view
       the mountain close behind.
Too warm to worry at obscurities,
as long as summer flourishes we find
       the proverb proving true:
without a qualm we put it out of mind.

Only when late October turns to later,
herding the leaves determinedly away,
       will it preempt the scene
like an omniscient, meddlesome narrator
blundering on to hog the stage between
       the high points of the play,
telling us what we're meant to think they mean.

It was impressive, seen the first time round:
barefaced, baldpated, raked by livid scars
       (inactive ski runs, those).
Under a paling sky, on chilling ground
we saw sustained this minatory pose
       and wondered if our stars
had something near and dismal to disclose.

But repetition blunts apocalypse.
We pondered less the second year's unveiling.
       The flinty interludes
are curtained off as winter's rigor slips;
and, knowing what the annual rote includes,
       we'll face it without quailing.
It's different with our own abeyant moods.

Cloudscape

To a man sick or in prison I imagine
clouds passing must be a comfort, bringing
rifts of distance into a room's sameness.
The June high pomp of their elephantine
processions, the autumn wind-disheveled
horse tails and manes tell the time of the realm.
Then there are all those protean tableaux
convincing to none but each expositor:
one man's duck is another man's dragon.
Only the other day I saw
Ely Cathedral serenely wandering east:
nobody else would have. Think of being
all things to all men, of having your silver
lining accepted all over as credit,
of being above it all. They have it easy,
or so it seems from this bow window where
I spend so much time following their maneuvers,
overcome some days by so massive and blank
a longing that it takes minutes to remember
that I am almost never ill and always free to go.

The Shortcut

A shadow scythed across the lawn.
I saw the shadow, not the bird.
So briefly come, so briskly gone
no salient traits could be inferred

except that it could use its wings
to a superlative degree,
to judge from those quick scissorings
that sliced between the sun and me.

This image cuts more ways than one,
I said to none but my machine
that labors loud beneath the sun
to shave the ground a level green.

That shadow, aimed at beckoning shade,
lanced beyond reach of burning day—
while I with mine, blade matched with blade,
hacked out a path the longer way.

Turn, Turn

The sprinkler swings a veil
of feathered rainbow half around,
then with a meager wail
as of a rust-encumbered hinge,
turns back again to trail
its wondrous, sun-bedotted fringe
across the damp, appreciative ground.

To look becomes to listen.
The water, whirled and atomized,
applauding its own glisten,
fosters a bright din amid the grass.
Rusty, though, afraid of being risen,
hope waits for a spigot's twist, alas,
to dry up all that eye and ear have prized.

Out Back in the Evening

Noticing now how trees in twilight gather
closer, more in command than you know them to be,
snags the eye on advancing time foreshortened,
jostling top-heavy into your modest plot.

As if a signal—could it have been the porch light?—
beckoned them nearer in, a noose never yielding,
or as if twenty years' growth had come
upon them in the blink of a wearying eye. . . .

It goads you on to envision the day when noon
will show no brightlier than the summer dusk,
when the damp grass you stand on and the benighted
folk in the house will not have known for years

days when the sun would pour unbaffled down.
If you came back to it then, could you manage to care
as bitterly as you do in the noiseless fall
of dew, strange to a place you know each stone of?

Past time to go in. By the back porch steps
the cat claws up at a glitter he can't ever catch:
bright eyes, fireflies, hunter and hunted, alike
innocent of foreboding, at home anywhere.

Note Found in a Room in a Summer Hotel

If there were an empty bottle handy, I'd
be willing to commit these words to water;
but there's a little left in mine, and I
will no doubt need it where I'm headed for.
To whom it may concern, I'd like
to pass along some observations based
on a profoundly uneventful stay—
uneventful but averse to efforts
to rinse it out of mind, a mottled stain
lingering out of reach above the tideline.
I seem to have been here all too many times,
though not in recent years: the robin's egg
tint of the walls is fly-specked to my sight.
The wide-armed rattan rockers creak
under my window, the old Yankee dames
creak almost as much when they stand up.
They know what they like, and it's all here for them:
nubby white bedspreads, white abrasive towels
a bit too small, no TV noise, no air
conditioning, nothing to jar with the "nice touches"
the management forty years back was noted for:
that clamshell soap dish, that tooth glass
with lilies of the valley round its rim.

The first morning I stood here by the window
a ball of yarn, a shocking crimson clot
launched from an unseen lap beneath the roofline
unreeled until it halted under my eyes.
Minutes went by and no one picked it up.
Dead or asleep, I thought, and turned away.
If you are sensible and look out, not down,
you see why people pay for such a window,
a sunny gable blandished by sight, sound,
and smell of the sea. Should you perversely pull

the rubbery green shade down on all that view,
leaving the ocean's paced impetuosity
to its own loud devices, there remains
the wall calendar tacked up near the washstand
with its expectable lurid aqua seascape
ready to wave you back to time and tide.

Am I unreasonable? The bed's not bad
(and I should know, my back
being my most sensitive part but one).
But I suspect it of inducing dreams
I'd rather not have had, unraveling time—
I am, unhappily, a child again.
By main force my father yanks me blubbering
under and through each cold, concussive wave,
trying to teach me something in his way,
suddenly parted from me with
a wave of his vanishing hand,
terror breaking to empty strangeness when
the sea I fight alone turns into sand.

My mother figures too in these adventures,
a step behind me on the sunny boardwalk,
letting me lead, although I'm small enough
to walk in the nodding shade of her coolie hat.
We come to a fenced, round pool where every day
a pair of amphibious girls, one blonde, one dark,
wheedle a pair of dolphins to jump through hoops.
Gray arcs of muscle bursting from out of sight,

they break the sequined water like torpedoes
and are again gone and again in air.
I feel a hand on my shoulder. Then I don't.
How shall I turn, knowing her there no longer?
Spray drenching my knuckles leaves them numb.

So much for each of them. But couldn't I
dream them together? Once I did: a lone pair
propping each other up on one
beach quilt with another shrouding their knees,
wordless, sipping coffee from a thermos,
passing binoculars back and forth
though no sails were in sight. They had grown old,
with awful suddenness, and at last
were smaller than I was, while I watched
from some invisible vantage point.
Speech was beyond my power, or possibly
hearing was beyond theirs—otherwise I
would have forgiven them everything for ever.
Late in the season, late in the afternoon.
The sun falling behind their backs
spilled a current of blood across the water.
They looked at it unblinking. I could not look,
closed my eyes, which curiously enough
led me to open them onto this dark room.
That was my last night here. I've no regrets,
only wonderment that I should have come
to get away from it all when all the while
so many things are getting away from me.
(The airport bus, if I don't move, may do that.)
You, tossing socks and so on in a drawer,

remember, as long as you're here your time's your own.
I hope you knew at this time of the year
it chills off in the evening pretty sharply.
After I read this over I'll bump downstairs
with as usual too big a suitcase and
commission those knitting widows on the porch
to make the next sweater mine. That ought to kill them.

Coast Patrol

What does it mean, miles from any shore,
October coming on, three mornings running
I wake to blink away a stretch of beach,
trackless until, there! the truck comes putting
along on tractor-style tires, and hands
heave out coils of hurricane fence on cue.
One pumpkin-orange spool per hundred feet
lands with a thump and rattle, heavy kindling.
The truck drums out of sight, its arrowhead
cipher of tread inscribing unpaced sand.
Impatient to wake, I loiter between the tracks
peering ahead to where they appear to meet,
then up, to see a sky unrolling streaked
and haggard as though dragged through an acid bath.
Then seaward, where no canvas gathers wind,
then closer round, where metal-mesh refuse cans
squat like empty cages, upside down.
Even the gulls have gone home.
Too late to be lifeguards, when will the crew come back
and unwind wire and wood and plant
their prosy barrier to prevent the dunes
from slouching off in the general exodus?
Coming awake always before they come
I rub the sand that escapes them out of my eyes.

Contemporary Music

The neighboring wind chime we have never seen
tinkles its giveaway through shifting gaps
in our imperfect barricade of green,
teasing its audience from hammock naps.

These aleatory noises that the ear
makes, if not music of, at least a mood
no doubt say less than we are wont to hear,
their antic peals agreeably construed

as hymning summer's gentle dispensations.
When life, too long immured, moves out of doors,
this jingling ushers us to recreations
adjourned by only flower-primping chores.

Ringing its tintinnabulary changes
on all the whispered fluencies of air,
the half-a-dozen tones it rearranges,
taxing to score, might register somewhere

between a cowbell's ruminative clatter
and thinner clinks of silver-pitchered ice.
We wonder what fine-tempered bits of matter,
launched in performance randomly as dice,

are joined in this ensemble: Venice glass
dangled in sleek medallions the sun loves?
Or, from Korea, some shell-casing's brass,
by second firing made a flock of doves?

This latest thought slides glumly into place
just now, as bombers on a training run
boom out a bass line, lumbering back to Base,
their mettle advertised, their duty done.

When all in aftermath has fallen still
we wait, impatient for the pliant chime
to play at whim, or at the wind's odd will,
keeping no time except for summertime. . . .

And so it does—but sounds far less emphatic
after that squadron's passing tore the sky;
a brief emergence from a blare of static.
Twisting the mind's dial, can't we try

to render dominant those frequencies
where only mild-mannered tunes are played?
But signals waver; summer's touted ease
is stricken mute beneath that droning shade.

Old Burying Ground

As long as men have cleared these fields of stones
this spot has been a portion set apart
for those who cleared them to inter their bones,
their names indebted to the carver's art.

Here sanctioned graven images adorning
legends incised below their low relief
feature in turn for every era's mourning
a choice device to give a shape to grief.

The elders ordained skulls with bear-trap teeth
hovering gleefully on harpy wings;
their sons, more civilly, repose beneath
the cherub's less aggressive flutterings.

Their grandsons, still more decorous, enjoyed
an emblem classical in its reserve:
a willow with despondent boughs deployed
to frame an urn by their condoling curve.

Marking the measured ebb of holy dread
drew smiles from these prim and bulbous *putti*,
till they absconded, leaving in their stead
lachrymal limbs to do their pious duty.

Was this the destined course of intellect,
the forfeiture of faith for sentiment?
Heaven left faceless, how can we detect
what even that third generation meant,

festooning their commemorating lines
with such pathetic shaggy dogs of trees?
Trite as their trusted proverbs, these designs
planted in rows present a pallid frieze.

Did they imagine this entablature
graven with sorrow fountaining afresh
might be a means for sorrow to endure,
perpetuating tears among their flesh?

Or had their Yankee caution coldly weighed
the likelihood their latest heirs would keep
a living vigil? —Once the bill was paid,
the willow could be counted on to weep.

Half-Holiday

       Off for the afternoon
and lounging brightly on a bedroom chair,
the summer dress, a flower-sprigged affair,
lets dangle folds that lazily balloon

       their acquiescence in
the huffed behests of an impulsive breeze.
The whispering, brisk avidity of these
over-the-sill transactions seems akin

       to cravings I could name,
ready to ruffle with their mock-sincere
sighs the most mild, untouseled atmosphere.
Call the wind wanton, innocent of shame,

       see him desert a sleeve
after a wistful twitch, fade back to flirt
with curtains, then surge in to lift the skirt,
having his way in one concerted heave,

       exhibiting in graphic
pantomime acts of mortal bliss and folly.
Should a faint, stray influx of melancholy
mingle with this inane, promiscuous traffic,

       let's credit the old Romans
with true discernment of the querulous dead,
rising at noon to envy the lives led
by offspring no more apt in reading omens

       than they were in their day.
Eddies of force in starved pursuit of form,
ones whom the sun at zenith cannot warm
well could be moved to haunt that soft array

       draped to incite a glance
to grow into a close, consorting look.
And that, of course, is really all it took
to set this model free for dalliance,

       freeing ourselves likewise.
Let randy zephyrs and regretful shades
pant for embodiment, their escapades
scarce noted since our own exchange of sighs

       sprang up an hour ago.
Ventings of this world and of that unseen,
blank to what mysteries of substance mean,
hanker in vain for knacks our bodies know

       of giving life to grand
alliances we toast adherence to.
Fireworks garnish fetes of much ado.
Keys of the city pass from hand to hand.

       No need for now to dress;
a casual spirit reigns, and rules that we
owe the loose shift extended liberty.
Long may it wave, inspired by this largesse.

Things We Will Never Know

What became of Krishna
the blue point Siamese
strayed *circa* Nineteen
Fifty-five in Levittown

Or the box turtle Churchy
lost a few years later
What seduced them away   Where
is Jimmy Hoffa   Judge Crater

What was the name of the dwarf
newsboy we used to buy
Sunday papers from for seven
years until we moved

Who were the Cardinals named
in pectore by the dead Pope
What's in the Fatima letter
Why did Lester leave the Church

Why did his wife leave him
Why didn't she leave him sooner
What made him drink like that
How much did the children know

Who built Stonehenge   Why
Where do the Gypsies come from
Did Cranmer really carry
his wife around in a trunk

Who was it with a smoker's cough
that kept us jerking awake for months
How could walls have been so thin
When did they tear that building down

Who burned down the Reichstag
What is the Great Sphinx watching for
What have we lost for ever when
the shy dream edges away

What do we look like when we sleep
When it's done with who will come
to close our uninquisitive eyes
and make the arrangements needed

Chronometrics

I. *Turning Back the Clock*

      By setting back these hands
I win an extra hour of sleep tonight
and make each winter morn a shade more bright.
      Seasonable demands

      within our sphere are met,
while nothing will draw short or slow the arc
the planet orbits through an ordered dark
      whose clock but once was set.

      Between the time we make
and that which makes away with us—the sun's
cold strategy—our hot resistance runs
      through snow for summer's sake.

II. *Digital Clock*

The days are past when people might
mistake me for a mean night light,
an exit sign, a smoke alarm.
Consider, should I fail to charm:
The circle you no longer see
has been economized in me,
a billboard changing as you blink,
diminishing your need to think
of hours past or yet to come.
The dial trailed by pendulum,
the water's lapse, the shifting sands
defer to digits. Look, no hands.

III. *Grandfather*

They stood me up, a coffin in a corner.
When no one volunteered to sound a knell,
I lifted up my hand, a willing mourner,
and let my chime supply the passing bell.

Many a midnight since I've kept my vigil
seconded by the moon upon my brow,
who changes phase and face to suit his schedule.
(His grinning sickle profile's peeping now.)

Such years I've given to this undertaking
I have forgot for whom these rites are done.
That rueful wooden clack my tongue keeps making
would serve to usher onwards anyone.

IV. *Hourglass*

Belled at top and bottom, pinched at the waist,
I move this little desert I've encased
whichever way is down. Its thin descent
mounts to a dune by steady increment.
Once multitudes convened to see me perch
at preacher's hand in each conforming church,
and as he schooled this world to meet the next
I mimed his arid sifting of his text.
No sermon runs an hour now. Nor do I.
Shrunken in stature, wrested from on high,
I time a mere three minutes for your egg.
Nothing like time to take one down a peg.

V. *Clepsydra*

By steady, sedulous embezzlement
I drain the minutes only to let flee
my liquid gains whose loss I then lament
with marks left high and dry inside of me.

At bottom I'm a leaky drinking cup
whose fill, for ever listing from the brim,
must tantalize dry lips to siphon up
sips to endure this rainless interim.

Drought is the fixed condition of us all,
in exile from the everlasting springs.
The used and ruthless droplets I let fall
mimic the shimmer of the tears of things.

VI. *Sundial*

Bent-headed one, can it be time to linger
    watching my gnomon trace
the daylight's path with one black, pointed finger
    while soldered to one place?

Having become a shade you will not cast
    a shadow men can see:
rove in your three dimensions while they last,
    and leave the fourth to me.

Moss

Not so much groundcover as groundhugger,
it beds down between the tough knuckles of tree roots,

or crowds the crevices in the unsunny side
of a garden wall, cosying up to cold brick,

or fills in after the thin, indecisive grasses
that limp through summers under the long arbor.

Prospering most below notice, staking claim
to nooks that most green lives grow feeble in,

it's made of reticence a choice career;
and to the overshadowed man who rubs

his palm over its pile it hints of mild
delinquencies: the level felt of billiards,

or barbered turf laid round the eighteenth hole.
One man it reminds of a velvet piano cover—

green, only brown in spots if you stroked the nap,
hanging in swags like a war-horse's blanket,

in a grandmother's parlor how many
mosses ago he would hesitate to say.

Partial Draft

My ear, still keyed to summer, failed to label
a murmur stirred by the mild October day;
so, lured at last mid-sentence from my table
(What was the word I wanted?—It slipped away)

I turned to see how, eased of my attention,
trees turning fast had scattered half their load.
What I was hearing, mind in meek suspension,
was former foliage hurrying down the road,

a fibrous faint grating, skip, and bustle
made when the wind dispatches lemony shoals
over the asphalt. That doom-eager hustle
whispers a dry subversion to the souls

of those still undisposed to follow after,
intent to stay awaiting a later word.
A second wind: cicada-like but softer,
the sound is known this time when it is heard:

a noise more near to silence than most noises,
bordering silent moments when the pen
upon some puzzling brink or line-break poises
before pursuing its scratchy path again.

Last Winter

That was the first snowfall
of our last winter there,
a single inch, neurotically
exact in depth and spread,

more a job for a broom
than a shovel or perhaps
not even worth bothering with
after the sun came out.

Cast at an angle, siftings
were caught in every link
of the steel fence's diamond
mesh, and briefly glittered

diamond-like in melting.
By noon the gauzy shawls
slid from the black roofs.
It lingered on the longest

off in a dim corner where
loops of weed were poking up—
worried threads that pucker
the nervous child's quilt.

Then, out of place as irony
that hadn't quite succeeded
in furnishing the emphasis
the situation needed,

that patch dissolved as well,
enlisted in *les neiges d'antan*.
The later, deeper snows
we hardly noticed, too

busy with packing up.

Homework

In those last years she sewed mostly by feel.
The window by her chair did little for her;
late in the day she felt the sun lowering
and went on stitching, nodding with the rhythm.
It was a finely honed accomplishment,
something she took grim pride in. It was only
threading her needle that she needed help with.
Then the boy would put his book down and try
to spirit through the niggardly steel loophole
the slenderest of ends, which in his fingers
bulged as coarse and clumsy as a hawser,
butting the aperture it aimed to pierce.
The little eye itself would seem to wink
maliciously, repelling his rude stabs.
The thread slipped through at last as if by luck,
or in derision, finding its own way.
Slowly, with practice, he got better at it,
returning sooner each time to his homework.
Sometimes he wondered: what could it be like
to watch the prodigal spectrum of the world
narrowing like a peacock's closing fan
until, all suns extinguished, it became
a dull swag drawing lines across the dust?
He thought of how, years younger, he had played
tourist in his own room with his eyes shut,
coming so quickly up against a bedpost
that he gave up, disgusted. Patience came later,
partly learned from the one who sat each evening
lining her steady rows of stitches up
against the dark upwelling. When he looked
up from the page at her in her dim corner,
then quickly back to it, his eyes would blur:
as if the graphs and characters he studied
had bled their precious ink to turn the busy,
columned page a sudden, solid black.
Then he would blink, and bend to the next problem.

Accidents

Speed came to a stop here, suddenly.
The lamppost, now a shade atilt, withstood
the meeting better than the emptied car
whose front end, once a grinning width of chrome,
is crumpled like a quelled accordion,

whose windshield is a wide-cast web
of glinting shock threads I imagine
tensing without end to catch
in one shivering net the shreds
of what is left of all our lives:

we have gone through the glass.
I haven't seen you for years but I remember
your dream as if I dreamed it: out alone
in deep night, wandering blocks you couldn't number,
casting your eyes from side to side and finding
every window broken,
every window broken.

What's to be learned but wild tact to walk
around these badly lit collisions sown
witheringly thick in space and time?
Now, even as I watch,
two barefoot children laughing under the eye
of God or God knows what jump past
the scatter of glass and run away still laughing.

// II //

Echo

You here again? Of course, I should have known:
spring outshouted you with a chortle of
nest builders and nonce rivulets cheering the sun,
summer covered your calls in vibrant green.
Now when bewildered trunks, crown-scattered, stand
ranked in chorus ordered to be resonant
of loss long to be borne, you sound among them:
Here! and again Here! But where is Here?
Before, behind, the winter-hollowed woods
offer you alcoves as I lean and listen,
wondering what first sent you wandering, sad
Effect for ever yearning to meet and mate
with callous Cause, likely not worth your while.
In the pause after the period your poor would-be
rejoinder hangs in the breathing space, more inquiry
than answer, ever aggrieved to hang unanswered.
Further words, while the voice holds, defer
your making known your wavering whereabouts;
but silences entice you nearer home,
as I have grown to know in shortening days
hard by a brook gone mum with ice, my ear
locating you at last so close you might
after all be huddled in its crimped labyrinth,
murmuring Here, as I hear and again hear you.

Circumlocution

Footsteps, measured, almost a dead march,
going nowhere within four walls,
overheard almost every evening.
Wearing holes in the carpet, my
grandmother used to say.
Threadbare itself, the old phrase
springs with a strength I would have thought
long faded on me as my eyes start up,
almost at once realizing, oh,
it's only the housebeams settling.
Settle down: why nag the ear now
to follow that circuitous trail
coming at last to climax with
the squeak of a desk chair's swivel joint,
the toy railroad rumble of
its iron wheels drawn up to the big desk's kneehole.
It was my cave in the mountains when
he wasn't up there writing. Writing? Walking.
Thinking on foot, one old man's way
of not wasting paper.   What he called
"the circular file" had little of his in it:
neatly opened envelopes, mostly, the month's bills.
I used to look at their cellophane address windows
and wonder why just *people* couldn't grace
their correspondence with transparency.
(This was before I could read.)
The three-cent postage featured profile busts
of the Founding Fathers, wigged and sphinxlike,
some looking left, some looking right, all looking dead.

Lagging a fingertip along the mock-
Moorish perforations of its rim,
on summer afternoons I clung to the cool
metal round of the wastecan, breathing in
a charred smell of emptied ashtrays that
tinctured scraps with a derelict, downfallen
air, the unmistakable stamp of trash.
Or I climbed into the huge chair
to look at the paperweight—a glass globe;
inside, a single penguin keeping vigil.
His eyes were ink dots, for a beak he had
a snowman's bright, aggressive carrot nose.
Stiff-flippered, he stood always at attention.
Shaking him up produced a satisfying
blizzard for a minute. If the light was right,
I could see my shadowy self blinking
back at me from the clouded crystal's surface.
There were no papers, ever, anchored down
by this ensphered antarctic scene. I thought,
"That must be what the penguin's waiting for."
As for me, what I wanted
was a desk like this someday,
which now I have and at which now I sit,
saving a little paper, throwing out more,
seeing and hearing things, not writing, waiting,
writing again, waiting for the right sounds.

Some Methods of Going to Sleep

After the clock is wound and the lights are off
some, unconcerned at seeming quaint, still pray;
some rehearse color schemes or street addresses
of all the apartments they have ever lived in
since leaving home; some reckon in their heads
all the loose change the day took from their pockets;
some count cars going past, or not going past,
whichever there are more of. Your routine
or mine, small rites for tamping down the day,
grow from a grain of faith in things unseen,
or glimpsed between lids ready to acquiesce
in the absorbing darkness. There are a few
phenomena to be counted on, or just counted;
peace lies in knowing tomorrow will be Tuesday,
or that no matter how many willing integers
march by in single file disguised as sheep
there will be more to lead you on to sleep.
Should rituals fail, or lists, or attempts at setting
meaningless words to a tuneless patter of rain,
you might try telling yourself a story as long
as it would take to lose all but the one idea:
say how a sea captain's children every night
watched their mother's finger steering a course
across a chart that filled the bedroom wall,
through unpronounceable straits to open water,
finding a point in all that pointless blue,
on which they came to rest, from which they drifted
off into sleep at her saying, "There he is."
—Something along these lines, until, your eyes
quiet at last, she's gone to sit downstairs
a little while longer. There she is.

There and Back Again

Black from the poker's soot,
the thumbprint plants a maze
on this new leaf turned over.
The tired man whose thumb
provided this exhibit,
pondering the cunning whorls
can picture venturing in—
shouldering a way between
carboniferous canyon walls
cast in a dismal grid.
There at the shunned center
he'd end up face to face
with what? Some horned and hoofed
incumbent hot for slaughter?
Once I might have thought it.
Now I believe he'd find
only the lost child
long ago left behind,
waiting among the ash heaps
for someone with the nerve
to lead him out of there.
Half-asleep, the boy
has propped his chin on one
or another grubby fist.
He hears a step, and stiffens.
The time to go has come.
Alive to every risk, the late
but always destined escort
is foolhardy or smart enough
to trust as compass only
his own wincing memory for
the many steps they'll take, reversed,
to be outside once more.
The way out is hard.
They lose count of the blind

alleys just avoided,
charred crimps and turns.
Somewhere—they can hear it—
a whispering fire burns.
But there it is, the final gap:
beyond it, both are free
and fearless, the man standing
stunned by the sudden whiteness:
just when could it have snowed?
He drops the boy's hand to see him
run wherever he will—
no sentries. Now he wonders
why at the grimed, outermost
wicket gate did no one
straddle the path, demand to see
what some would die to flourish:
proof of identity?

The Voice of the Yawn

Bodiless though I be, if you ever could track me
down to my dark impenetrable den
in which I huddle dormant between forays,
you'd stumble over me located somewhere near
the bottom and back of the brain as it tapers
into the spinal stem, the unlighted crossing
where thought and what you like to call "being thoughtful"
descend to the brutal honesty of reflex.
It's there, when the fit is on me, that I first
make my embarrassing stirrings felt,
touching off my powder train of convulsion,
by an obscure, incessant tickling
tensing your neck and tightening your jaws,
inciting, as my dark urges burn
to declare themselves, a humid, bulbous
exhalation to occupy your mouth,
demanding to be let out or swallowed;
and as your eyes narrow and mist with tears,
your cheeks flush with propriety's exertions,
you know my power and know that not to yield
will only invite the return of the repressed.
I wish that I could predict, any better than you,
just what is needed to trigger one of my tantrums;
sermons hovering round their halfway points
are a safe bet; most any reasoned discourse
in fact runs the risk of my putting in an appearance.
Reason and all its works and I are at odds:
I am not thoughtful toward you, anyone, anything.
You ought to make the best of things, throw back
your inattentively nodding head, spread lips and let
me issue forth in operatic splendor.
You might come to cherish me for my social utility,
your faithful, misshapen dwarf of a jester
whose grotesque somersault into your waning soiree
will send the stubbornest guests in search of their coats,
end the long evening, get you to bed at last.

Safe Harbor

Past midnight, and much darker
than when I hit the pillow,
I heard the channel marker
appraising every billow
whose overweighted crest
collapsed with all the rest.

Its single note, dividing
the shallow from the deep,
took on the task of guiding
me out again toward sleep,
loosing the stubborn painter.
The port lights playing fainter,

it braced me past the bold
breakwater that takes the pulse
of tides in pincer hold,
a final perch for gulls.
It tolled me seaward, till
it too, becalmed, held still

and the unfathomed sea
again made room for me.

Spring's Awakening

Oddly assorted bedfellows, frost and thaw
ruckus under their scanty quilt of clay.
To them, spring comes as the final straw.
Their tortured nights are pictured plain as day
in sudden humps and craters that we find
in garden ground upheaved and undermined.

Tossing about, all elbows in the cramped
embrace to which their restless kind are fated,
their lust for loamy struggle never damped
in all the years since they were strangely mated,
neither has known the other's throes to yield
to careless calm. Their bed's a battlefield.

Curious: what they fight is what they share—
a sullen trance where serial nightmares reign.
Scouting the damage spades will soon repair,
shouldn't we feel less ready to complain?
Our cruelest dreams have yet to match the girth
of these, that wrench the surface of the earth.

The Floater

They always used to say, demanding elders,
schoolmasters in manner or in fact,
that this boy was a hopeless drifter, lacked
direction, drive, and didn't give a damn.
Floating face to the sky on a summer lake,
not getting anywhere fast, he called to mind
calmly the old reports of still no progress,
and knew them true—years, years had passed,
and here he was, the flagrant foil to their
frustrations which he could not make his own.
And there was no excuse. He hadn't been there
to watch his father running to catch that train,
only imagined the platform-edging gravel
galling the knees, the loaded briefcase tumbled,
the fingers popping off the collar button.
Some people can't relax to save their lives.
Arching his back on water's ample roundness,
marveling how it will just as soon uphold
a hippo or a splinter, he felt drained of weight
and curiously transparent, like a teardrop
gliding across a wide unblinking eye.

The Invention of Zero

Arithmetic's anonymous Hindu hero
altered the sum of things by adding zero,

ushering digits upward place by place
to scout the outer curve of outer space.

Immensities of distance, mass, and weight
came to be prey and play of chalk and slate,

bane to our sophomore doodling his exam.
Can't we inspire him to a dithyramb

on powers compact within the simple o?
The world itself was made *ex nihilo*.

Acclimatizing

A blue spruce, transplanted,
may not remain true-blue;
hydrangea petals, litmus-like,
will vary in their hue

from here, of sky at sunset
to there, of sky at noon.
Flower and fir grow color-fast
by slow turns until strewn,

besting attention's bid to span
each deepening tinge of change
until they've worn unwelcome out
in soil they came to strange.

They mock at man uprooted.
Could acid soil or base
lend him the local tincture, thus
determining his place?

Not even if he stood the while
to watch his footmarks fade
would earth exert its buried might
to modify his shade.

The Crossing

Leaping the stream I wished
some memorizing eye
or touch quick at a shutter
could have composed us there,
upheld for a marked minute
us hand in hand midair,
while underfoot the flurried
colors of our flight
flocking on the water's bright
mimicry of sky
would slacken pace, the hurried
current cease to flow,
and time shelve awhile its dry
demand for what we owe.

Call it a peak experience—
over before we knew.
We stood and looked around,
calling the cloudless day
too good to be quite true.
Birds and a mild breeze
passed murmurs in the trees,
but otherwise no utterance
came from the neighboring wood.
Brought down to earth for good,
I soon took hold of sense,
knew that the sun bound westward,
air wavering, water fled
were not our elements,
and knew that now we'd found
our feet on solid ground,
we had a ways to go.
I said, "We'll take it slow."
You said, "Why shouldn't we?"

Early Natural History

The girls his brother brought
down to the beach that summer
were different every weekend,
but really all the same:
cinchy, giggly blondes.
He couldn't be bothered to notice
just which one it was now
fresh from the waves and dripping
(they always did) all over
today's baroque sand fortress.
They were worse than dogs that way.

His castles stood the grandest
as far as he could see:
extravagantly buttressed,
turreted, topped by jaunty
paper-straw flagpoles.
His massive moats were filled
with bucket after bucket;
impregnability
was what it was all about.
Drops from her sopping hair
were melting away a cornice:
"Stay over the moat," he yelled,
"if you have to stand and drip."
She giggled and walked away
with his brother, equally wet.
He heard his brother say,
"It isn't the waves you have to
worry about, it's only
the undertow"—a thing he said
to each wet girl each weekend.
They left him to his repairs.
He watched them walk off laughing,
the late afternoon sun

throwing their pipestem shadows back
across the reddening sand.

He thought they were all just chicken.
The Undertoad—he was only five
and it didn't scare him a bit.
It only came out at night,
breaking the sea's black mirror
just at the turn of the tide,
searching the deserted beach
with eyes globed and dirty gold
as the family Packard's headlights.
Two hops brought it ashore,
landed it in a baleful squat
athwart his helpless bulwarks.
No defense against that.

Up in a stuffy, resinous
bedroom under the eaves,
behind the dunes, almost asleep,
wrapped slack in the warp and woof
of all the sounds of the house
(footsteps up and down stairs,
whisperings, muffled laughter)
some nights he thought he heard it
rising above the sea-boom:
the croak of spite and triumph—there!—
as the walls came tumbling down.

Their Voices

I used to hear them late at night, the voices,
back on Saturdays, back in that neighborhood,
down below, loudening out of the distance,
blurring away again before too long.
There was a lot of laughter, not very bright.
Now and then a few lines of a song.
I would remember words, notes, if I could,
some little souvenir of some lost night,

but nothing now survives for exact quotation.
I lay on the long dimming edge of sleep,
heard them scuffing the gritty curb of manhood.
They talked about the girls they'd been to see,
or what a motherfucker Charlie was.
Through chainlink fence, exhaust-afflicted air,
and dusty leaves of a lone ailanthus tree,
all this intelligence filtered up to me.

So much more than a couple of city
blocks, lots, and storeys stand
between us now, my nights have grown
so quiet of late with certainty.
Here in a time of too much known for sure,
I wonder how it would be to hear their voices
rising free and so soon falling away,
stupidly happy, ignorant of the choices
made for them long ago, long nights before.

Blues Remembered

Plastic chairs anchored
in boundless cement:
the War Memorial Auditorium,

Boston, back
in the middle 'sixties—
is time, is place a part of performance?

Old Son House
could hardly carry
himself, let alone his guitar onstage.

Lighting was no more
subtle than the decor.
In a white shirt he was high-grade coal.

He sat a minute
limbering till
his fingers loosened. Then played like hell.

Once, between numbers,
he looked down at us
and said in a voice like a spade raking gravel:

"I love Gawd.
I love everybody.
If you got religion you know what I mean."

No one said a word.
Then a girl giggled.
We clapped, embarrassed, and waited, blank,

for him to lift up
slag-heavy hands,
to span and grapple with steel once more,

to play a song
whose words, half mumbled,
would cover up silence. At last he did.

Ash Wednesday, Late Afternoon

Dust-motes bustling up—or is it
in, or through—this afternoon's
lazily sloping chute of light
seem intent above all to scatter
havoc along the grand
avenue that irradiates
their antics, unprogressive, up *and* down,
I now see, tracking one or two
only to lose them soon in the lit swarm.
Inflamed with no mere ardor now to rise
but at whatever risk to swing and shine
in these remoter reaches of the sun's decline
they do, in fact, dazzle as they conduct
carnival turns and vaults in bliss above
their stunned confederates thickening on the carpet—
the fatal plain to which they too
will settle. Don't they know it? When they do,
they will have lost their audience, hung
in cooling air, the sun's last ladder rung
tweaked from beneath them, finding this to be
an unappreciative arena where
the act winds down after the spotlight's moved.
Their ultimate stunts, in graying vacancy,
are dartings we can take only on trust,
picturing that deserted turbulence
dimly subsiding, mating dust to dust.

Souvenir

He'd thought that they were through,
this man making his bed,
until he happened on
a single strand of hair
left by her lying head.
It bridged the pillow's dint,
unnecessary hint
of one so lately there,
grown restless now and gone.
It robbed light from the sun.
He wondered what to do:
initiate witchcraft
upon this mortal thread,
unreeling force to find her,
impel her home, and bind her?
But then he almost laughed,
realizing that the one
adequate spell was hers,
and that when all was done,
said, or let slip unspoken,
he was the quarry caught
and fettered by this token,
held, as he held it, taut
above the disordered bed.

A Late Greeting Card

They won't grow older, ever.
From them my quick tongue learns
each year to save its praise
on their outstripped birthdays.
Their many happy returns
led them at length to Never.

Things that I should have said
then, when the hour was apt,
then, when a willing ear
would have been keen to hear,
I stack beneath the rafters, wrapped
and earmarked for the dead

too sharply distant to receive
tribute with easy grace.
As far beyond the speed
of sound as beyond need,
they leave me laden in my place
and cannot give me leave

now to make good the gaps.
So the words stay unspoken,
bright undelivered gifts.
Some day when the wind shifts
and the attic panes lie broken
I'll auction them off, perhaps.

A Time Piece

for C. F. S.

Again, the daily swing.
Your flashing, clamorous arc
grows wider as you grow;
your high delighted hum
startles the sleepy park.
On from the fast-decamping snow
and puddled green of spring,
it's been our place to come.

More than a year old now,
all day you're on the run.
Later, the rocking horse
and rocking chair likewise
will certify your day as done
by cantering through their course.
The days are laced with cold now;
gold leaves excite your eyes.

At last the swing hangs plumb.
The motions of your day,
the evening's hurried blue,
sway even me toward sleep.
In earnest as in play
may I keep time with you,
the only pendulum
that gives me time to keep.

Morning Exercise

>   *for A. P. G. S.*

My son assists me shaving.
On a laundry hamper lid
he sits, big-eyed, behaving,
watching the busy skid

of blade leveling stubble
his chin has yet to sprout.
An urge to be my double
is what it's all about,

and so I lend him lather
(there's plenty for us both)
to play at being father
while I cut back on growth.

I notice, bending nearer,
the decades' detriments,
then try the kindlier mirror
his upturned face presents.

Admiring how intently
he pares his suds away,
I view my flesh more gently.
Now for another day.

Finding Words

Candid will be my word for you:
one of my words, when the time has come
for summary, for my stepping back
to see what it was I held.

Candid as light that imparts to every
vine-ripened gourd or willow wand
its hue and heft, sun-plumped or of windy
pliancy, inviting the hand,

or even before the hand's adventure
inviting the answering light of the eye
to linger upon its prodigies.
Or culling over the elements, I might

call you candid as water taking
its calm and fluent time downhill,
smoothing a cobbled bed with cool persistence,
showing sky a responding face.

Candid as earth, I'd say, that waits for
water's encouragement, fall when it will,
whose dust expectant admits no loss
of landed dignity in a dry season.

Air that will bear words chosen and spoken
quick to your ear will be an equal figure.
Even in silence it cannot be empty
to eyes that have seen how sunlight fills it.

That is the clarity language looks for,
finds a word for, and makes it serve.
I can be candid too if I call you
all that an apt word grows to mean.

To the Next Tenants

Although we even dusted,
and did our best to leave
no hoard of homely relics,
you're bound to find a few:
the rest of a roll of tape,
a couple of plastic cups,
in a back bedroom closet
a brace of bare coat hangers
dangling like ascetic bats
designed by Giacometti.
The lighter patches on the wall
will say where pictures used to hang
(always a bit too high).
Otherwise, you'll discover
only the idiosyncracies
of a house freshly emptied:
the way a floor, uncarpeted,
can look ablaze in daylight,
while windows without curtains turn
a glazed and jaded stare on that
impounded, breathless fire.
Cover them for your peace.
In the first days you'll notice
sounds that quickly enough you'll be
comfortably deafened to:
the tick of wind in the chimney,
or, less elemental and more
often, there's the second
step from the top that offers
invariably a wry comment:
"Oh, so it's you again"—
my wooden paraphrase.
That really is about all;
we took an inventory.

Our shadows and our echoes
have gone away with us;
you'll bring your own, and welcome.
The rooms burn to be filled.

Just Here and Now

I couldn't give any reason for slowing down,
just here and now, bedazzled by a solitary
mailbox you could see from half a mile,
a loaf of white heat. Half the summer might go by
without its red flag ever perking up.
Coming closer now tugs into view
the ragged patch of chicory it stands in,
bent spokes of petals dusted by wheels gone by.
The fence behind is here and there missing a picket
as if a dog determined to be playful
had run off into the orchard with it.
From here a drive more dirt than gravel rises
past a barn that hasn't seen paint
in God knows how many years,
up to a turn-around where three or four cars
(it's hard to count) continue patiently
to rust in various states of disassembly.

Why have I stopped? Just possibly, because
nothing is here that is not plausible.
It's hotter by the minute.
The house can just be seen between the shade trees;
that must be the kitchen window.
Yellow curtains. Without a doubt, inside,
a spool of flypaper twirls from a ceiling light,
and doesn't ever manage to catch enough.
The floorboard cracks have long since come to be
a crucial part of the linoleum pattern.
The oven door hangs like a drawbridge down.
How could anyone bake on a day like this?
But the older daughter is just done icing a cake.
She hands her small sister
the large spoon to lick.
And nothing could be more proper:

it is the little girl's birthday.
(How do I know? I just do.)
Being nine at last has gone to her head.

Looking out the window,
she sees the blue roof of my car
and wonders when they'll take her to see the ocean.
She pops the spoon in her mouth
and sights along the handle
like Daniel Boone drawing a bead on a squirrel.
Like all of us, she loves to make more of less.
She is lost in the sweet wonder of seeing double:
two windows, two mailboxes, two
cars stopped for no reason there on the road—
until her sister, seventeen, so much taller,
tells her for it must be the twentieth time
that if she won't quit crossing her eyes they'll stick.

MANKATO STATE UNIVERSITY
MEMORIAL LIBRARY
MANKATO, MINNESOTA